VANISHING
IRELAND

VANISHING
IRELAND

PHOTOGRAPHS BY
RICHARD FITZGERALD

TEXT BY
EDNA O'BRIEN

Clarkson N. Potter, Inc./Publishers
DISTRIBUTED BY CROWN PUBLISHERS, INC., NEW YORK

Dedicated with love to my wife Louise,
my sons Giles and Michael
and daughters Anna and Maria,
for their support and patience
during my many absent hours and
frequent stops along the roads
of Ireland.

R.F.

Grateful acknowledgment is given for the excerpt which appears on page 18 from "Under Ben Bulben" from *Collected Poems* by W. B. Yeats. Copyright 1940 by Georgia Yeats, copyright renewed © 1968 by Bertha Georgie Yeats, Michael Butler Yeats and Anne Yeats; A. P. Watt Ltd. on behalf of Michael Butler Yeats and Macmillan (London) Ltd. Used by permission of Macmillan Publishing Company (New York).

Published in the United States of America in 1987 by
Clarkson N. Potter, Inc.,
225 Park Avenue South, New York, New York 10003
Originally published in Great Britain by
Jonathan Cape Ltd.,
32 Bedford Square, London WC1B 3EL

CLARKSON N. POTTER, POTTER, and colophon are trademarks of
Clarkson N. Potter, Inc.
Manufactured in Italy

Library of Congress Cataloging-in-Publication Data

O'Brien, Edna.
Vanishing Ireland.

1. Ireland—Civilization—20th century.
2. Ireland—Description and travel—1981–   —Views.
I. Title.
DA959.1.027   1987   941.5082   86-20509

ISBN 0-517-56508-0

10 9 8 7 6 5 4 3 2 1
First American Edition

I invoke the Land of Ireland
Shining, shining sea.
Fertile, fertile mountain
Gladed, gladed wood.
Abundant river, abundant in Water.

A huddle of people and myself waited at Newbridge Station in County Kildare to catch a train to Cork. The day was bright and of an extraordinary lustre. In the sun the black crows seemed like spools of satin let loose into the sky and the ivy circling the gashed trees had the appearance of frosted Elizabethan ruffs. The people stood, quiet, shy, so self-effacing that they seemed to be eating the inside of their cheeks to cover up their embarrassment. Not a voice was raised. That is one of the things you first notice, the soft-spokenness of the people and often the equivocation that goes with it.

'I'll ring you maybe.'

'Do.'

'I might come back tomorrow or I mightn't.'

'I'll try and meet you.'

'That's if I come.'

'Do you know what you'll do … if I don't hear from you tomorrow I'll probably hear from you the next day.'

'Probably.'

'The same applies to Wednesday.'

'I tell you what. The best thing is to see how you get on and then ring me.'

All around there were posters proclaiming Friendliness in Ireland. Tradition in Ireland. Travel in Ireland and History in Ireland. To emphasise these qualities there was a picture of a church, a white cottage, a dolmen, a lady harpist, a fiddler and a cloudless blue sky.

A young man striving to be punk had a gold sleeper in one ear and half his face sheathed by a spill of purple hair. There were two ladies with him whom he zealously tried to offend by sulk and silence. Yet as the train pulls in he kisses one of them lightly. The party who had

been endeavouring to make a plan exchanged farewells that would not go amiss if one or other was boarding a coffin-ship to America.

'Tell him I was axing for him,' a lady shouted, as she helped her hefty friend up the high step on to the train. Svelte figures were not greatly in evidence.

Inside the train everything was spruce and clean, with a most marvellous smell of rashers and eggs. Why does travel make one so heartily, so giddily hungry?

In a sense it was not travel for me. I was coming home to the country of my birth, the country I could hardly claim to have left, since it occupies so much of my thoughts and a great deal of my fiction. The old emotions started up – pity, exasperation, heartache, the need to flee. Growing up in Ireland is unlike growing up anywhere else. There is more emotion per square yard than there is rainfall. That has not changed, at least not in the country, where the attachment to home and hearth is as deep and as binding as the longing to escape it.

We were crossing the central plains – over it all a sense of space and timelessness. It is sky and field with banks of hawthorn hedge, followed by more field, more hedge, then at intervals a herd of cattle around a feeder, so stationary that they look inert, dried frozen dung like bristle on their haunches. A country of profligate beauty known for its religious fervour and for its prowess in breeding thoroughbreds. It is a great thing for a small country to excel both for her own sake and as a refutation of history. It is not that there is an active animosity towards England or for that matter towards any foreigner but the instinct of desperation dies hard and the Irish have a long memory. These are the qualities that create writers and Ireland has had her share of them. I looked at the clouds and thought of how

5

Joyce described them: 'the muttoning clouds'. I was thinking also of Maria Edgeworth and her book, *Castle Rackrent,* which charted the fate of a ramshackle house and its several owners, who, though all different, had one trait in common – profligacy – so that the house went to ruin. Thackeray was inspired by it to write *The Luck of Barry Lyndon,* another saga of affliction. The landscape is full of reminders of *Castle Rackrent,* ruins, broken walls, avenues with briers over them, large gaunt edifices with the wind keening in the upstairs chimneys, shutters askew, tongues of flowered borders hanging from the ceiling, beautiful editions of old books clogged with damp, frayed silk cushions, a turf fire and everything in direct and blessed contrast to that most puerile of English tendencies – cosiness.

No, there is nothing cosy about Ireland: the clouds rampaging; the sheepdogs, many of them blind in one eye, tearing after motor-cars; and the whole notion of protocol distasteful to a race in which each believes himself descended from a chieftain but tricked of his proud heritage.

Of course the roof has to be repaired, central heating put in, and to effect this some owners of mansions have opened their great ballrooms to the startled and loquacious citizens of Tennessee and beyond. I was not there to witness these hectic visits, having chosen to travel in the winter to see what J.M. Synge called 'the grey and wintry side of many glens'.

Hotels closed, hotel owners fled to the Canaries, bed-and-breakfast signs creaking and squeaking over iron gates and the hunting season just begun. Clare was asleep till Easter...the whole country was asleep, but Dublin, where I had spent a few days, was awake and agog with all the old gossip and malice that the city is renowned for. Such and such a widow was having a great time of it, looked twenty years younger, another lady who had an illegitimate child wasn't letting on whose it was – it might have been the curate's but it just might have been a literary man's. Dandies who live by their wits sliding up to you in the hotel lobby, saying you look 'delightful, delightful'.

My first rendezvous was with a man from the transport office who gave me brochures and a free train pass.

'Now secrete those about your person ... I can put you on to people who will give you a good steer ... meet some old biddy or other and that'll get the poetry into your book. All you have to do is put your ears about. The guy that's going to drive you around Cork, he'll be a medium-sized chap with kind of ginger hair and he'll be waiting for you beside a steam engine, some kind of antediluvian thing that they hawked out for a centenary and never put back.'

In Dublin on the Sunday morning I walked along the streets listening to the bells and the odd holler from one side of the road to the other.

'Good morning, great and yourself, had you a late night, have you the rats?'

In the shop doorways there were dossers smothered in coats and plaid shawls, with the empty Guinness bottle to one side. The various bells summoned the worshippers to God and an English colour supplement showing Robert Redford on the cover was blazoned everywhere because Robert Redford's father, like James Joyce's, hailed from Cork, and hadn't Robert Redford often publicly said that he would make a film of the great dashing invincible hero Michael Collins? Dublin, however, was not where I would find the dream of Ireland or the remnants of that dream, what Yeats called the 'dance music of the ages'.

When I asked the guard on the train if he could spare me a few minutes there was at first a smile, then a baulk, then suspicion followed up by the excuse that he had better not, as he had to keep going. To my great surprise he sent his assistant who arrived with a first-aid box, asking if I had injured myself. Hearing that I was eager for a chat, he asked if it was trains I wanted to know about. 'No – life,' I say, recognising the absurdity of such a generalisation. Off he was on a verbal canter. Two bridges had been built in Cork, costing well over a million each, of which the EEC paid a big whack, a rich American had bought a beautiful castle with a herd of white deer which he has to thin out every season, and Fred Astaire the film star came to the Blackwater River. The Blackwater is the second longest river in Ireland, it rises in Ballydesmond and goes to sea at Youghal. Since I was going to Cork I would be able to eat Drisheen and Coddle.

'Drisheen is a mixture of different bloods and different herbs.'
'What's Coddle?'
'Everything and anything.'
'How do you mean?'
'It could be bacon or meat or anything you have handy.'
'I see,' I said, not seeing.

We passed a town with a graveyard on the hill above it and the tombstones tall and starkly white, like joking lanky sentinels keeping guard over all. We had crossed the plains and now there was the beguiling sight of hills and mountains, the blue and the brown and the purple that gives Ireland her special radiance. I was hearing about patriots and priests. Thomas Davis had been a native of Mallow, he who had written 'A Nation Once Again' which would be the anthem of Ireland when we got the six counties back and were what we should be – a united Ireland. Out of the town now, the hills and the fields like slices of marble cake, brown, green and lilac, some fields lodged with water and others with the grass in biscuit-coloured tufts. Besides the poem, there had also been a song about Mallow and the rakes who used to go there to take the spa waters, but now the water is polluted and the song an echo of times past. Times past permeate one's consciousness whenever one sets foot in Ireland.

However, as he reminded me, Mallow has a thriving sugar factory plus a chocolate factory, and nearly every house has a television.

'What do you think is the influence of television?' I ask.

'It highlights the robberies.'

'How do you mean?'

'People don't leave their doors open any more at night.'

Robberies led us to vandals and eventually to drugs.

'Three girls get on the train one day, and one of them goes up to the dining car and gets a cup and asks to have it filled with hot water. They were sniffing out of the cup, when someone smelt it. I didn't know what it was but I marched up to them and took the cup and threw it straight out the window. They started screaming at me, two of the guards had to come to my assistance. We quietened them down, we said we'd report them.' It could have been floor polish or aerosol or some kind of glue.

'How long have you been on the railway?'

'Years and years.'

'Twenty years?'

'Maybe more.'

'What else do you remember?'

'We were stopped one day and I went over to one of the vans and the fellow inside shouted, "Don't open the door." Of course I didn't.

Then he said, "It's OK – now you can open," and he had a goose – he was putting her into a sack. He brought the goose home and the children made a pet of it. Come Christmas Eve he said to his wife, "You'd want to be killing that goose." But she wouldn't kill it. It had to be brought next door and given away. The woman next door killed it, but none of the children would eat it because it was the pet goose. Another time we had a derailment and I had to drive the cattle out of the wagon and along the road to the next station. I had five cattle to start with, but when I got to the next station there were fifteen. 'Twas a dark night; I don't know where the other ten came from.'

A man stalking the corridor, eager for conversation, butted in. The guard called him doctor to his face and something else behind his back. The man said he was a lawyer in the morning, a travel agent in the afternoon, a fisherman at weekends and an engineer beyond in London three days a week. He said that you couldn't make legal money in Ireland so he made his illegally and that the City Hall was spelt Haul because of the way they roped in the people's money and that all the councillors were imbeciles and that the only reason cremation was frowned on was that these hoboes knew they would be roasted on the other side. His own pet vengeance on the world was particularly reserved for the transport company; whenever he got a chance he put his car right up to the snout of a CIE bus so that it couldn't budge and the passengers went up in arms. The English were very nice people and there was no reason at all to take issue with them and wouldn't we have been fried in some concentration camp if we had been in Europe, in fact we didn't know how well off we were, to have England as a neighbour.

The 'dear old aqueous' city of Cork on its reclaimed island waste. I passed the hotel where the crotchety Carlyle took a rusk and a chop and where Maria Edgeworth and Walter Scott were gazed at by all. I saw roughly the spot where Parnell stood, pale and bearded, between the tar barrels and the torches, to be hailed ten days after he had been stoned at Enniscorthy for his adultery. Further on, Drawbridge Street where the rebel Lord Edward Fitzgerald had to get up from his lunch of mountain-fed mutton and French claret because the British squad were after him. Here Spenser married and Walter Raleigh governed, here also are the finest hurley players in Ireland and it is thought the cutest businessmen – the Jews of Ireland – and the bells of Shandon, the sound of railway yard and dockyard, the winding streets with names like Friary Lane and Butter Lane and Christchurch Lane: a city that has a certain chauvinism in itself and more loyalty than any place else in Ireland.

The evening clouds were like lakes, lazying along the heavens, lakes of blue and black and flamingo pink, and the crows here, as elsewhere, assumed they owned the road.

It was on from that, to a surprisingly pampered night in a hotel which boasted a Michelin star. Farmed *huîtres beurre-blanc*, medallions of salmon in saffron-coloured sauce, *pommes dauphinoise*, sorbet to freshen the palate and a conjecture as to whether the wine was too petulant or not. A kitchen, as well run as a missile base, with every kind of machine: machine for plucking the pheasants, machine for making the ice-cream, making the sorbet, a vivarium for the oysters, shallow pans of water ready to cook the vegetables, urns of pea soup with their bottoms raised in order for the air to circulate,

château this and château that, the jelly from the veal bones glistening like frog spawn and a surprising hush as each person attended to his or her task.

Out in the garden there was a white stone sculpture that was somewhat suggestive.

'Is it a breast?' I asked the waiter.

'It's nothing else,' he said, a bit embarrassed.

The owner – with a culinary dedication as intense as Patrick Pearce's – delighted in the fact that when anyone laid eyes on the sculpture their bad minds started to work so that he had held a competition as to what it should be called and the best answer that came up was 'Stoneage Bra'.

In the lower garden was the strawberry tree, or the Arbutus, a botanical freak in those parts.

'Can you eat the fruit?' I ask.

'You'd eat one but not a second one,' I was told.

At the other end of the room a man was trying to make his point known in a manner that could only be called vociferous:

I thought it was demeaning
I thought it was insulting
I thought it was boring
I thought it was shite.

And whatever it was that had heated his blood, he went on denouncing it because never, in his own estimation, would he be sufficiently heard or understood. The national trait, a craving to be heard, in a country that is short on listeners.

I had unwittingly achieved what Marcel Proust always insisted on – a whole hotel floor to myself. It was in Kinsale. 'Eight hundred reasons for visiting this sailing and gourmet resort,' the brochure said. The gourmet side of things was absent, it being off-season, and the swans in the harbour were able to glide up and down without interruption from boat or yacht. Two flags, Canadian and American, fluttered in the cold, a token of the one and a half million visitors who came to Ireland last year and who were most zealously awaited this year and next. I was within a few miles of the place which became a scene for prayer, hymns, vigils, conviction and emotion when a five-foot-six cement statue of Our Lady of the Immaculate Conception moved, opened her hands, shed tears and did everything to confer with the faithful, bar speak. I was certain that the people would be eager to talk about it but instead there was caution and even reluctance. The women who most fervently believe in the Virgin and in the profundity of the phenomenon meet each evening to say the rosary and to make up to Mary for this hedonist world. Nothing can save Ireland except constant prayer.

'You see, the prophecy said a big bird would come landing on the earth,' said one woman; this she and others took to be the Indian jumbo jet which had crashed in the sea and which, unless the praying is intensified, is an augury of the end of the world. Birds have always been auguries in Irish legend and mythology. A black bird for harm, a bright bird for good:

> God for his comfort sent a flight
> Of birds angelically bright
> That sang above the darkling lake
> A song unceasing for his sake.

She said that it was marvellous how God took people by the hand and brought them to prayer. She herself was unceasing now, with litanies, rosaries and ejaculations, which she said all the time while making the beds in the hotel, walking to and from home, and more openly when she convened with her friends in the evening. I asked to meet some of the women who had seen the statue move but they all declined and I think it is suggestive of a new thing that has happened in Ireland. In the desire to be modern, not to be a laughing stock to the rest of the world with a 'pigs-in-the-parlour' image, Ireland has decided to become matter of fact, to become guarded. She does not want to consider the supernatural. Miracles do not exist. A sense of wonder is on the wane. The clergy do not want it to seem that Ireland is still in the Middle Ages. The young girl, whose sister first saw the statue 'moving like mad' in July, says she didn't go down for nights, she wasn't bothered. The stories written about it varied, from mockery to dry scientific speculation – the autokinetic theory, the hysteria theory, the hallucination theory were cited again and again. Also an impatience with it: 'People were going over the top or sending others over the top. Faith was not to be confused with superstition and grace was not the result of some piece of hocus-pocus.' There were jokes – people had pinned signs on her: 'Out to lunch' or 'Back in ten minutes'. People had defaced her, Protestants or Jehovah's Witnesses from Dublin had gashed her and she had had to go back to the factory to be repaired. But despite all the carping, the excitement – or the relics of excitement – lingered on. A public telephone had been installed near the grotto, along with two lavatories, which one man quite understandably regarded as a miracle, albeit municipal.

It brought crowds, it brought business; it is thought to have effected two miracles, although one is in doubt, because the lady who so dauntlessly threw away her stick at the foot of the grotto was later seen on crutches in the market town. The moving statue, or, as they termed her, 'Madonna on the Move', was a boon on two counts – it brought the attention of the media to the place and it brought people back to prayer. The fact that they came in busloads, month after month, demonstrates the hunger, both for novelty and for the supernatural. The fact that the priests have to be wary and even dismissive about it means that they too recognise the hesitation that is in the faithful.

> Babe Jesu lying
> On my little pallet lonely,
> Rich monks woo me to deny thee.
> All things die save Jesu.

For many reasons – poverty, television, brashness – the soul of the older Ireland is being trampled on, in the interests of a new, drier, more matter-of-fact, bureaucratic, religion. Also a schizophrenia about the faith itself and those who minister it. I was told that priests mix with ordinary people now, and that a priest at a wedding in Limerick had his hall-door out and did everything bar ask the bride to go to bed with him, and that another priest in Connemara had written a book in Irish about a priest getting a girl pregnant and that he hadn't been de-frocked or even cautioned. This need to be tolerant has induced a brashness and a farewell to both wildness and innocence. There are no surrogate Christy Mahons in either street or farmyard and if there were they would be given tranquillisers or electric shock treatment.

Exaggeration and wonder are on the wane. The great floating psyche that feeds literature is being put to sleep by a new kind of philistinism, less rabid than before but more insidious. An Irish prime minister once remarked that he didn't see why he should let dirty books into Ireland, any more than he would let in dirty meat. Everything pours in now, but the interest in literature is moribund. Literature that used to be regarded as a sin is merely incidental, an unnecessary luxury. Videos have replaced the written word and every girl I talked to was addicted to *Dynasty*.

I went at dusk to see the Madonna on the Move, not knowing what to expect. There, at a bend in the road, was a huge grotto and the heroine herself perfectly restored in her niche, a crown of lights above her, the head tilted a fraction to one side and a red carnation stuck in between her clasped hands. It was neither wishful thinking nor simulation, but the statue moved, moved so turbulently and so cosmically that I was sure she would fall. The movement went on and on, making one think at first that it was some kind of mechanised

performance and then that it was coming close to farce. The local young man with me said it was the first time he'd seen her move and that he'd never forget it. There we were in the evening light, the night sky above us, and this piece of cement appearing to want to convey something of drastic intent. I had no idea what caused it and when I came back and sat by a forlorn gas fire I read a book on the matter which told me everything and nothing. I was glad to see her move, not because it brought a great resurgence of faith but rather a fleeting return to childhood, to that particular state of openness and expectation. I thought of what Yeats said about art, about its being childhood and death and the great affections and the orgiastic moments. Turning from that to another potentially orgiastic moment, I perused in a brochure the duties consequent upon a wedding for the bride's mother, for instance:

Arrange printing of invitations
Send invitations
Order wedding cake
Order wines
Hire photographer
Florist for church and reception
Order cake boxes
Arrange display of presents
Hire cars
Contact local newspaper for announcement
Arrange entertainment for the evening
Hire video company

The following morning, in the window of a shut shop, I saw a postscript squeezed in between fishing tackle and Our Lady calendars, a motto which said 'Not for Sale'.

> Before marriage – he talks and she listens
> During the honeymoon – she talks and he listens
> After the wedding – they both talk and
> the neighbours listen.

Plans were afoot for the summer festivals to Pan and many another god. A young girl was painting a picture of the French flag to accompany a flourishing 'Bienvenue'. Most urgent of all were the schemes and preparations for a flower festival that was going to be called 'Entente Florale'. Meetings were convened; flowers, shrubs and trees were to be planted depicting the maritime history of Kinsale and her heroes who fled to Europe where they were known as the Wild Geese. Flowers were to hang in boat-shaped baskets, more flowers serving as frames for yet more ingenious arrangements. A lick of paint everywhere, sparkle, enthusiasm and a plea to rise early on the day. The committee were urged to get the judges to Kinsale by seven-thirty in the morning when the town looked her best. A leaflet emphasised this point; it said 'No joking. Continentals won't be at all surprised and we can get up early for once.' Souvenirs in the shop windows and on the cluttered shelves alongside the bawneen jumpers and the ponchos. Mementoes that would make Mr Yeats turn in his grave, though not Mr Joyce, he being of a more humorous and astringent disposition. There were Innisfree perfume atomisers, forty shades of green paperweights, laminated posters of Georgian doors, copper book-ends, lambs and sheep sculpted from marble chippings and a rocking sheep complete with off-white fleece. In the papers the new American ambassador proclaimed 'the joyous dimension of her calling', bringing with her the love of 44 million Irish Americans and being just thrilled to be allocated to this little slice of heaven. This little slice, which, alongside Greece, is the poorest of the EEC countries and where welfare recipients constitute one third of the nation.

"Tis a cool day, 'tis indeed, I didn't let you know I was coming, my experience of leaving a message is that things tend to get distorted, so I thought I'd come myself and show you around.' On that breathless spate of greeting, we set out.

My guide says he is not a very hectic driver and then proceeds to berate all other drivers, who indeed deserve his opprobrium as they pull out of side-roads and bohereens without as much as a beep and then glare and shout abuses at those to whom they have caused fibulations. 'We are going to see a bridge over which stone balls are pitched once a year, an event which brings a gas crowd. Presently it appears that we have gone astray. We stop to ask directions from some road-workers who are beholding a bulldozer. The question is passed from one to the next and then the next as if it were a password. Eventually we are bombarded with rather bewildering directions and the man who gives them concludes by saying, 'Are ye happy with that?' as if it was a piece of fiction which, considering the next hour of hithering and thithering, it most certainly was. However, the driver was not bothered, there being no chance because of the weather to do any farming – his other occupation – and he regaled me with stories of scandals, embezzlement, wife-swapping and suicides. 'A fella gave a lift to a young hitch-hiker and when he was getting out the fella said, "I'm going off now to kill myself," and he did, he drove the car over the cliff. Had I heard the one about the tinker who wandered into a hotel to answer the call of nature on the night of a fancy dress party and was mistaken by the doorman as one of the entrants? Lo and behold didn't he win first prize, which was £50 plus a bottle of whiskey.'

I ventured to ask him why he thought the Irish drink so much and drink to get drunk. Without as much as a qualm, he said it was because they were so confident, much more confident than the English or the French or any other race. Invincibles. A more inaccurate observation I have never heard.

When Thackeray travelled from Cork to Skibbereen in 1842, he took a four-horse coach called 'The Skibbereen Perseverance' for which he paid the sum of 3/6d. The coach was full to the brim. He wondered what it was that made these restless Irish people hurry from one place to another.

The morning I boarded the bus at Cork Terminus there were just four other passengers: three ladies and a gentleman back from England holding a bottle of duty-free gin. We were a fairly silent party who settled ourselves in separate seats. The silence was due partly to the cold and partly to the fact that the bus jolted so much that it was, as one of the ladies said, 'like being on a horse' and that 'it would shake the guts out of us'. It did.

Thackeray described the ride as desolate and bare, yet beautiful because there was a set of hills to keep one company most of the way. Carlyle went there too, and oddly enough his description seemed more accurate: 'Bog round us now, pool and crag, troublous hugger-mugger aspect of stony fields.' Carlyle did not care much for the Irish, any more than Thackeray did. The shock of seeing such appalling poverty, hovels and people in rags, wrung from these two savants opprobrium rather than pity. It is hard to think of a man of Thackeray's tenderness feeling neither pity nor shame for people so destitute. He did not acknowledge that England was the extortionist: 'Ragged women chattering and crying their beggarly wares, ragged boys gloating over dirty apple stalls, fish frying, and raw and stinkin'; clothes booths where you might buy a wardrobe for scarecrows, black gaping windows, women with bare breasts nursing babies, ragged children paddling everywhere.' The poverty that Thackeray saw, and that was to be hideously and indeed calamitously worsened by the potato famine five years later, is not so extreme now, but the loneliness is certainly still there. In Thackeray's time the population of Ireland was approaching 10 million, and now it is just over 3 million. Looking through the window at the odd isolated cottage or a woman driving a few cows or a man carrying a bucket, you get the feeling that they're indefinitely cut off, on the edge of the universe, that even Cork is an eternity away – not just in distance but in its way of life. The *huîtres beurre-blanc* and all the attendant delicacies seemed a whole continent away.

As we neared our destination, the woman in the seat behind me confided that she had been in Dublin with relatives for three months and that she was a little daunted at the prospect of coming back to Skibbereen, where diversions and hobbies for women were few and far between, unless you went in for dinner dances or ladies' football, neither of which she fancied. The bus driver took two side routes, simply to drop each of us at our journey's end.

When I arrived at my hotel I had that sinking feeling that befalls one on entering a cheerless abode. A sign for Mass and a Church of Ireland service were pinned to the side of the reception desk, cigarette butts filled a little black grate, and left over from some function, possibly a wedding, were small posies of withered and discoloured carnations. A man was dozing in one of the big gaunt lounges. Nothing but big lounges whose only concession to chic were carpets of immense and worrying garishness. There was also a high chair for a baby, and some preparations afoot for a dinner dance which was being held that night.

Thinking it best to have a few gulps of air, I repaired to the town to see what life was like on a busy and bustly Friday afternoon. The ladies' couture in the shop windows was not by any stretch of the imagination resonant of fashion. Indeed the dresses were, as the man said to me elsewhere, 'bend minding'. Impossible partnerships of lurex and tweed, leather and taffeta welded into an ensemble, and hats, knitted, pleated, dented, swathed in gauze – all proclamations of such folly and such boldness that it was as if every woman in Ireland wanly dreamed of being Scarlet O'Hara.

Down the town, towards the monument for the martyrs, were wellingtons at keenest prices, whole sides of beef fresh from the slaughterhouse, with the vets' blue brand of approval on their creased skins, hanging up in the window to tenderise, and another sign – 'Give Blood – Play Rugby'. The bone setter, who had come in from out back to do a bit of manipulating, was sound asleep at a counter, a warm mug of coffee kindly put beside him. Across the road in the record shop, a ballad was belting out, and the shop itself a tiny booth, covered with photographs of Madonna – 'Sings like a VIRGIN'. I wondered whether it was the implication of her virginity or her blatantcy that made her Queen of Skibbereen and more copiously displayed than that other Virgin. Young people came and went, asking the price of this or that but buying nothing. On the outside door, guarding the suggestible Madonna, was a fairly crude picture depicting the Last Supper, with an impatient Christ surrounded by girl-like, mendicant apostles. A motto said: 'Keep me, My Lord, from stain of sin just for today'.

That very day a shop which claimed to sell everything for under a pound had opened in an arcade. Business was brisk. I bought two jotters and a pen and asked the owner what he would do when he ran out of knick-knacks for under a pound. 'I haven't a clue,' he said. You wonder how they go on, and how for the most part they maintain this absence of anxiety, a fact evinced again and again by their unpunctuality and their trust in God about the wobbly morrow. In the street a boy selling the evening paper kept telling his distempered dog to relax, relax. Back in my hotel room, serenaded by the inevitable burps of boilers and the hum of machinery, I asked the proprietress if there was any way I could be spared the noise. She said she could hear nothing at all but that she always heard the people calling to her in their need. Religious ecstasy attended this declaration.

To calm myself, I unfolded my evening paper and, it being the eve of the Feast of St Bridget, I read an article claiming that St Bridget was beautiful as well as virtuous, practical, determined and kind. It was thought that she went around the country accompanied by a beautiful white cow, bringing blessings to homes and families. She left a ribbon on many a window-sill, endowing it with healing properties which were especially effective for toothache, headache, and women's ailments. Her flower was the dandelion, which was not only a vigorous plant relished by animals, but the leaves if blanched contained health-giving vitamins and minerals, the roots were a coffee substitute, the milky white sap a remedy for warts and the petals perfect for making a sparkling champagne-type drink.

Oh, for miracles! I went down to dinner with a certain élan and partook of something which Carlyle so brilliantly described as 'ambitious-bad dinner'. At the table next to me a Baked Alaska, as big and sprawling as a steamed goose, had just been served. Three people in the party took photos of it while the others commented on its beauty:

'It's so fluffy.'

'Will it fall?'

'We'll never eat it all.'

'We won't waste it.'

'Look, it's oozing.'

Otherwise a lull, broken only by the footfall of the proprietor as he noted the liability of each table and then wrote it in his little bill-book. The waitress kept saying, 'Everything all right,' without daring to pause for confirmation. I felt myself to be in one of those eastern-European hotel dining-rooms where all is stasis, where spontaneity is crushed by some invisible force.

However, I had no intention of airing the slightest little bit of disapproval, having learned from my paper that another hotelier had gone into a room at five o'clock in the morning, wakened a surprised sleeper – a member of a ballad group, reefed the blankets from his bed, demanded that he leave the room and then assaulted him.

It had all come about through a misunderstanding. Another customer, a publican by trade, gave evidence, telling how when he had booked into the hotel he had specifically asked for that room. As a regular guest he knew it was beside the toilets and as he had an artificial leg he wanted to be in a vantage position. The ballad singer, rudely awakened, refused to leave his room, the owner arrived, words were exchanged, fisticuffs followed and the legendary Irish shenanigans got underway.

The yell of Allah
Breaks above the prayer, the shriek, the roar,
Oh, blessed God, the Algerine is Lord of Baltimore.

In Baltimore they are proud to tell you that their seaport was plundered by Dutch, French, Spanish, English, Turkish and Algerian invaders. Pirates lurked there and smugglers traded in spices, tobacco, rum, elephants' teeth and embroidered bed covers. In the Sack of Baltimore a couple of hundred locals were taken as slaves to Algeria, a fact immortalised by the poet Thomas Davis, he it was who asked to be buried on an Irish hillside, without a tombstone but beneath 'green sods decked with daisies fair'. A half-ruined castle stands on the hill as a testimony to strife. The town itself has a pub which looks somewhat quaint, a huge supermarket and a new estate agent's. The locals think they might start a festival in which they would invite their erstwhile invaders to take part. Baltimore, like the rest of Ireland, is in sore need of money and impetus from the outside.

A few men sat in the bar pondering their pints, while a girl made toasted sandwiches in the microwave. It was like being inside a ship, the sea beyond the window, rough and rampaging, the walls covered with ships' mementoes – a caulking-iron, a wheel, ropes, duck lamps, compasses, binnacles, a brass porthole, propellers and sailing pinions. The customers comprised a Breton who owned a restaurant, a fisherman and a harbour master who was on call for the lifeboats twenty-four hours a day and whose office, not surprisingly, was the pub.

He said the place existed before Christ and had a tremendous history. Life was hard at the present time because the factory which made the trawlers had closed down and fishermen didn't make the money they used to, and the Spanish were fishing inside the limits and it was a devil to catch them. Baltimore seemed hard done by. There was not, however, the same pervasive melancholy that I had seen inland, but rather more self-sufficiency and an acceptance of their straits.

'We are governed by wind and tide and weather,' he said.
'The women?' I asked.
'The women too,' he said.

A sort of shiver went through me as I glimpsed for a moment the exigence and limitation of their lives, the dependence on tide and weather and very little in the way of change or diversion.

I had hoped to go out on one of the fishing boats, but the fleet was away; 'every damn one of them' catching herrings over on the Waterford side. I could come back in a week or two, when maybe they would be there, maybe.

'Are you a blow-in?' the man asked.
'No, Irish,' I said, but the fact that I live in England classifies me as a blow-in.

On the road over to Bantry the hackney-car driver dilated fluently and ominously on the state of the country and her tribulations: 'People want trendy places to drink nowadays, carpets and all that, but, God bless us, every young fellow that can is getting out fast, and a lad of my own is in San Francisco in the building trade and hoping to stay there because there's nothing at home, only two peninsulas of vast country with no grazing on them and factories closing down, going into liquidation. The liquidators have the best jobs. The factory for the fishing boats in Baltimore shut down and in Skib the one for the processed foods went wallop overnight. Wasn't there a computer factory all set to make the cheapest computers in the world, but an American crowd got there first and the Irish lost out? The thing is, they got too big for their boots: if you keep small you can survive, if

14

you spread your wings you're finished. The same with the builder fellow, he had all the big contracts and still he went bust. Farming, sure there wasn't any, because the farmers took the easy option, they went away from the root crops and got soft on the handouts from the EEC. Then, bad weather made the grass useless. Herds wiped out with hunger. Farmers not able to get any more credit from the Co-ops and, instead of calving, the cows were dying or weren't coming on heat. Atrocious altogether. The same with the youngsters. To be a young fella, a most depressing thing, walking around the town with nothing to do. They say to themselves they'll try London or they'll try America. Not a week goes by but two or three take the bus to England. It's not that they want to go…they'd rather stay at home, but they have no choice.'

The hills on all sides, girdling us, the clouds ominous and a Hurricane Betsy-pyramid of rubbish on a site which said 'No Dumping'.

To go from that to the patrician splendours of Bantry House is to have to slide one's mind as arbitrarily as in a dream. Beautiful Bantry House, with its fifty-two chimneys, and its rose drawing-room, with tapestries of the nuptials and toilette of Venus – made for Marie Antoinette's wedding, Sheraton furniture, Italian mantelpieces, Pompeii panels, Savonnerie carpets, a fruit market painted in part by Reubens, the arms and standard of the family, and a photograph of the present owner's mother, a Clodagh, in a long gown holding an ostrich as she waits to be presented at court. From the house there was a most spectacular view of the bay, the famous and much lauded Bantry Bay, and in fine and furious temper she was – 'Ah well of magic, sole sight of sea, green and livid as a serpent.' In 1796 here it was that the French fleet headed by Wolfe Tone was stuck in the most terrible storm and where yet another Irish rebellion was foiled by ill-luck and fate. The then owner of Bantry House, one Richard White, placed his home at the disposal of the British, which meant that the already frightened and demoralised French fleet could be routed. He was made a baron the next year for his pains and a viscount two years later. His son, who travelled extensively, sent shiploads of furniture and furnishings home from Europe. It is all still there. As I walked from room to vast room, each one replete with treasures and chests and trophies, I thought it odd, the dreams that men create for themselves – the rich stack themselves with worldly goods, the drunkard with drowsing potions, the ascetic with the hair-shirt, and for no reason I heard myself say:

I wake renewed by death
A shepherd's coat thrown over me.

Near by there was a craft shop, a restaurant for light refreshments, a restored wing, to be used for bed-and-breakfasts, and a considerable and disproportionate contrast between the gleam and grandeur of the staterooms and the more cramped quarters where the family now lives. Here was the most perfect paradox: the past preserved for, and indeed maintained by, tourists, the present existing as a shell of that past. The thought of having to have the fifty-two chimneys swept, the chandeliers washed and polished, or the precious Nabussa tapestries preserved from fraying, set me doing my sums and the owner had no hesitation in telling me what it all cost and how he just managed to make ends meet. A man of strangely mild and direct disposition, a realist, at last. He had transcended history, risen above any possible bigotry, bringing to one's attention the sad but sage fact that money is the bloodstream of life.

… an' your grandfather jumped up an' whipped down the loaded gun that was always hung over the chimney. He hadn't time to run out, so he just put his head up the chimney, an' let fly, an' be the time he had stepped out from the chimney down thunders as purty a golden-winged mallard as ever bate a wing, shot through the breast, and plunged straight into the pot of boilin' water, so your grandfather put the lid on the pot, hung up the gun, an' turnin' arund to open-mouthed about him, says, 'Boys,' he says, 'from the width yer gobs are open it must be a great hunger that's upon ye, so we'll make a male of this little duck in the pot before we go – feathers an' all?' He did so, bedad …

It was Sunday morning and the hills prior to rain had a grey threadbare colour. I was to attend a meeting of the hounds and harriers but was warned by my escort, a young girl with an uncommonly deep voice, not to expect big things, as it was a shoestring hunt, a bye-meet, since there was a counter-attraction over in Tipperary.

'Could be lousy,' she warned but added that we might get the old adrenalin up. I needed that, being jangled and unslept. The night before there had been a dinner dance held for the islanders and I, who had hoped to meet people who would transmit some of the strange wildness that J.M. Synge had found, was disappointed and surprised to meet a cannier breed of people. They came in their hundreds, with their heavy coats, plastic bags and droves of children.

'Nothing else to do,' was what one townsman said, referring to the offspring. Three fathers alone had twenty-six children between them, all of whom ran up and down the hotel corridors saying, *'tá se dorca, tá se dorca,'* (It is getting dark). The monosyllable had gripped this once loquacious nation – Great – Fine – Hi ya – OK – No problem. ''Tis a cool night. 'Tis indeed.' Conversation null at first until the tonsils get oiled – vodka and white lemonade for the ladies, Power's and pints for the men. The older men whom I approached thought I should talk to the younger men, they in turn passed me on to their wives who were addled, getting fizzy orange for their children to try and coax them to bed. The dinner menu was soup, followed by turkey with big dropsical mounds of mashed potatoes – and you bought your own drink at the bar. The speeches lacked sparkle, being long unending spiels about past achievements and possible future ones. It is the same with the newspapers, any regard to either the beauty or the particularity of language has been savagely discarded. The press resorts to a slang and a chumminess that is enraging. The people follow suit.

It was once they left the table and started the serious drinking interspersed with singing and dancing that their spirits rose. But by then they didn't want to talk at all and any man that I approached was certain that I had come in search of a quick fumble. Curiously enough the young women seemed to be more in charge than their escorts; the young girls looking both insolent and remote, as the men manifested their pent-up desires by much pawing and groping.

The radiators had been turned off, the proprietors being of the opinion that people's breathing would heat the place up. The older women fetched coats and cardigans to put over their shoulders and the men kept station at the bar, while an inebriate man recited a long rigmarole about a toothache. The monosyllable, again in the ascendancy – Great, Fine, Howia, Chock-a-block, Thanks, Dead cert. One man did suggest that if I lived on the island I would have the makings of a juicy best-seller, but when I asked for some details of the life there he loaded me with statistics. Literature is taboo unless the author be deceased, and then it takes on the mantle of history.

It was the same the next day with a young girl who was adamantly gun-shy. Even the simplest question yielded sealed lips through which only cigarette smoke issued.

We were waiting outside an office and food store – 'the wind making bullying rushes'. That was how those two dauntless ladies Edith Somerville and Violet Martin described the wind on a morning's hunt, and we were within miles of the place which they had described with such iridescence and such comedy. I asked my companion whether she had read the novels, but again there was a vigorous silence followed by a snort with which she implied that she did not care very much whether or not they had gone romping in the nude. Likewise religion did not worry her and she was so out of touch that on Ash Wednesday morning, seeing a woman with ashes on her forehead, she had taken it to be an Indian with a caste mark. She added that if anyone were to write about her she'd 'give out stink'. Suddenly without warning, she decided to turn the car, and the horse-box, around, and to tear up a deserted by-road. To our surprise we met a van, the driver of which shouted out to her to go to such and such a cross. She announced loudly that she was going to lose her top.

Eventually the meet had assembled. It was a fairly inauspicious gathering, comprising three huntsmen and my companion, all in the vilest of tempers.

'If I say such and such a place, I mean it.'

'Where the hell were you – at Mass?'

'Why can't you get your act together.'

'One and a half bloody hours in the freezing cold.'

Such were the rejoinders they flung at each other as they tackled the horses, treating them with sublime and contrasting gentleness. The hounds on leashes were baying so eerily that I remembered Somerville and Ross's description of this sound being like that of lost souls. My friend blew on her copper horn and they were off at such a speed that it was hard to know which direction they had taken.

I was being driven by a publican who himself hunted but had hurt his foot at a previous meet. Sitting in his car was like being in a refrigerator. The rain had turned to sleet and the barren fields were now covered with the merest glaze of white, as were the thorn trees and the little shivery bushes. At times he would stop the car and we would jump out in answer to the bay of the hounds. We saw them, lost them, saw them again, and it was the same with the riders, each of whom, to my inexperienced eye, seemed to be moving in baffling and uncoordinated directions. The young girl who had threatened to lose her top was obviously still in a lather, because instead of going through a gap in a fence she jumped higher up, giving her horse a smart kick and a few inimitable words. 'A flippant jumper' is probably how Somerville and Ross would have described her. For a few moments we had a fine view of the chase; hounds and huntsmen, just like a Brueghel painting, with the air as icy as Brueghel's drained green skies, and a sense of something thrilling about to befall. Then they were lost to us again, so we got back into the refrigerator and drove on, hoping to re-find them. In deference to my trade, the publican said he was not literary minded and did not read, but I need not infer that he was a dolt, because he only allowed the news or

documentaries to be seen on his television and forbade his friends or family from watching *Dynasty*. He then dilated knowingly on the weather situation, saying it would get colder, as it always did when you saw 'legs running down from the sun'. All I could see was my fingers turning purple and a windscreen wiper clogged with ice. We jumped out again in answer to some music as the hounds were coming near. Two young boys from the hotel were standing by the gate, giving the whole event their desultory attention.

'Thinking of taking up this?' the publican asked them, with a tinge of sarcasm. The frost on the gate seared one's skin and the only warmth in the whole world seemed to come from a series of matches that the young boys struck, as they struggled to light a cigarette. For no apparent reason my friend began to tell me in detail how the grey crows came down and plucked out the lambs' eyes just after birth. His interest in this was both rabid and clinical.

'Most likely they go for the softest bit,' he said, and laughed, and then hushed himself because the hounds, as he said, were giving great tongue and that meant that they must have risen the fox again. All conversation ceased as we spotted them going over a little field, quick and diminutive as birds, while in the next field a horse which was not part of the hunt galloped about in a frenzy. The hounds vanished from sight, only to appear once more, further uphill, murmuring like a flock of gulls. Again the fox had eluded them and, pointing to a thicket, the man said, 'She's gone in there, she's gone in there.'

No, the hunters did not wear red coats any more, because that was too much a symbol of the ascendancy, and it was bad enough leaping through farmers' fields and haggards without having one of them come after you with a manure fork. Everything was now more egalitarian: three of the hunters were Irish and the fourth was an Englishman who had retired to Ireland and kept his horse in the back kitchen which he had converted into a stable.

We lost them again and could not even hear a distant whimper, as the hounds obviously had gone inside a thicket of trees. We drove on and eventually found ourselves in a farmer's yard where a pack of sheepdogs made their territorial rights known. As we meandered up and down a few more nondescript roads, we saw the snow begin to fall, in quick slanting spills, and my companion decided it was time for his dinner. By now I was in such a state of arctic numbness that I could only thank God that I was going to be indoors somewhere, even if it was only beside a temperamental paraffin heater in a public house.

That evening I went to Castletownshend, the place where Edith Somerville had lived, to see the town and her house which, as she said, 'offered no compromise to beauty and made no secret of its contempt for the picturesque'. Walking up the street trying to find lodgings, I thought of a picture called 'She Drifted Rudderless'. It was one Edith had painted of her friend Violet going up a winter street in Hamburg in a cloak. I felt exactly the same as I searched for lodgings. In the end I found a place with an American lady who said I had thrown her for a loop by coming in the off-season, but that I could spend the night, and that she would put me in the toffee room and that she just loved my sweater and that her niece Shirley would love my sweater and that she would be serving for me crab for dinner followed by homemade blueberry ice-cream.

I sat on the bed and not for the first time pondered the cruel disparity between life and literature. I think it was Romain Rolland who said that art is useless against reality but can be a great consolation to the individual. The hunt had been something of a let-down; it could not compare with those which Edith and Violet had described – 'the glacial gleam of sunshine, girls in grey habits, the tumult of people on traps and bicycles, the wild sensation of jumping over stone and furze, the heady valour'.

Nowhere the spirit or the excitement of the crystal prose. It was the same in County Longford in the little museum devoted to Miss Edgeworth – a forlorn place with new sheets of brown paper covering gloves, satin boots, two irons, a lamp, a metrical exchange book and a canister for cloves, ginger and nutmeg. In the glass case two frocks of black and white lace. The woman who showed me around said she thought Miss Edgeworth was smaller, and that the dresses might have belonged to a friend of hers. 'They look a bit on the big side to be hers,' she said, as we stared at them. In Dublin James Joyce would recognise the solemn black door of Number 7, Eccles Street. Once guarding the abode of Leopold Bloom, it now resides in a fashionable restaurant. The woman who was dragging a duster over it said it was 'like an aul' tenement door' – the literary associations lost on her. In the Willie Yeats tavern in Sligo Mr Yeats would be offered sandwiches named after him, a fact which might perhaps give fresh indignation to his great epitaph:

Cast a cold eye
On life, on death.
Horseman, pass by!

And love and porter make a young man older
And love and whiskey make him old and grey,
And what can't be cured love, has to be endured love,
And now I am bound for America.

Four o'clock in a lounge bar in Kerry. A barrel of a man asks for a pint, then suddenly is letting out the most appalling roars and implications. He had been reciting a line of 'The Rose of Tralee' – 'In the far fields of India, mid wars, dreadful thunders' – when the distemper gets the better of him and the mutiny starts. He stalks among us, issuing the most woeful warnings, hateful glares, oaths and curses that could be heard at the far end of the hotel, bringing a scurry of staff as onlookers. He is now in full voltage.

'Keep back. Keep out. Don't come near me. Don't touch me. I'll kill the lot of you.'

We stood in a state of shock and some jitters as he rampaged, pausing occasionally in front of some unlucky face to deliberate on whether or not he should strike it. Eventually, and perhaps running out of steam, he burst through the swing doors, surprising a timid little man who, with a grin on his face and his hand out to cadge, almost permanently stationed himself there. On this occasion he cowered into his coat collar as the self-appointed cowboy went off down the street, telling all and sundry to keep back, keep out, keep away.

'Who the hell is he?' everyone asked, none claiming to know him or even to assume that he could be a native, though he most certainly was.

Back in the bar, the crisis was followed by a spate of intimacy and joviality, with the girl behind the counter repeating her mystification, describing how she had her back to him, how she was drawing a pint, when all of a sudden he went berserk.

On a high stool sat another man with a sack at his feet. He was fairly inebriated, but now King of the Proceedings, having the gift of the gab, or perhaps he had kissed the blarney stone which is sometimes referred to as blagarney stone.

'We're winning, proud of it, the name of the game, hello sweetheart, are you from Texas, thou'll wife is in jail for breaking windows, she's in for nine months, she can do it standing on her head, you know what courtin' is, I'd grab the arse off you up on the mountain.'

The assistant manager, passing through to ensure that all was tranquil, was at first amused, but suddenly felt it incumbent upon himself to deliver some advice.

'Christmas is over you know … you'd want to go home.'

'Home,' the man said, as if it was a jail or a lunatic asylum to which he was being banished. He ordered another pint and resumed his dotty monologue as everyone laughed and smiled, and the dull hours were for a time mitigated with the semblance of fun. In due course the disco would start up and a room more appropriate to Manhattan ('all the glamour and glitz you could ever want') would be lit with thousands of points of flickering light as the commercial travellers, sedate by day, tried to paw and wheedle the local girls. The girls, on for the flirtifying, were dressed to such a pitch of razzle-dazzle that one felt, indeed knew, that they wanted to stay for ever within the jarring fantasy world of the disco with its wild splashes of light and its strobes of effrontery. This is the nearest life gets to the *Dynasty* dream. In the morning it is back to the factory sirens, the church bells, and bread-men carting trays of cakes, cream buns and every conceivable shape of load into the innumerable confectioners. A sleepiness over the whole scene, somnolence, emphasising the fact that they are night creatures. The country may be at its most breathtaking in the early morning but not many are eager to see it then.

In the church porch a photograph of two priests in flowing white robes looking like Spencer Tracy. A sign that said: 'These are Dominicans'. A waitress from the hotel whispered that the 'Madman' had been pulled in by the Gardias, life was normal again. She believed in the old Ireland, went to Mass every morning, had a mincing smile and was the first to tell me one of the many poisonous jokes about the 'Kerry babies' scandal. Then a smile, as if to imply she hadn't said it. Butter wouldn't melt …

Inside the church the marble pillars, the gold leaf, a shivering Christ, the flicker of votive candles in plastic bowls and a dilatory sermon. On a second visit a few months later the sermons took impetus when discussing the topic of divorce; an evil which was compared with the ungaugeable disaster at Chernobyl. The inference being that divorce was not only as fatal as nuclear disaster but was also Communist.

Heavy snow had begun to fall. The slated roofs looked like houses from somewhere else. The Brandon Mountain with its cope of snow had all the majesty of the Himalayas. I was setting out for a jaunt in a pony and trap with my inebriate friend of the night before. He had promised to give me the low-down.

True to his trade, he had words of praise for all nationalities, then said that I seemed very educated and that I must be a schoolteacher. He decided to call me Edwina because he once knew an Edwina with a face like mine.

'Tallywack and tandem,' he shouted as he took hold of the reins, and warned me to sit well back in the seat for balance. The little cob, excited at the novelty of a journey in stark winter, set out at a dizzy canter.

'A brave gay morning it is, Edwina,' he said.

'A fierce cold morning,' I thought, wondering how long we would stay out and lamenting the fact that I did not see adversity as a source of inspiration.

'Jesus, we'll make a day of it like the gintry,' he says, as he swerved into a side-road, sensible from the point of view of avoiding traffic but perilous for the little cob who was without shoes. Hedges bulged and sagged under the weight of snow and the tiny fields were like virginal cubes without even a bird's faint track. The silence was so immense that one felt it would be possible to alert a friend across the sea in America.

'Make a wish now, girl, 'cos we're crossing a sthrame.' Then he expressed his own wish, which was to win the sweep, but countered it with the fact that health was everything, that health was a gift from God.

'You're handy with the pencil,' he said, as I wrote down some sage utterances, such as 'A friend is worth a thousand enemies'. He seemed disappointed because I was not a Yank, as he had a pile of cousins in America and more in 'Toranto' and born gentlemen they were and when they came in the summer they drove around with him and stayed out till all hours. For no reason he then launched into song, having a hoarse and tuneless voice.

'Very nice,' I said, to be civil.

'Christ, 'tisn't a song at all, only an aul' 'rincain.' He knew singers though, real tallywack ballad singers, 'Christ can they drink, they get sober on whiskey, they're so used to it and 'tis a bad drink, whiskey is, unless you have a cold, and sure this time of year you couldn't go long without it, 'tis like hay to a horse, and yes the country had picked up a pile, and there was good dole and sure the money crowd come in the summer, mad about Ireland because 'tis frightful old, 'tisn't in book or paper how old it is, but that there is nowhere on God's earth to beat it.' Other homilies followed, such as that the Irish are easily led but can't be driven, and that the wind does be fresh in the mornings.

We passed two people, Germans who were out for a constitutional and whom he hailed with lavish and loving expostulations. Soon after, a bungalow with 'Chien Féroce' on the gate, a fact corroborated by the bounding arrival of four snarling and primeval dogs, who avalanched upon us with a venom that sent the poor cob teetering to her knees. We had to get out of the trap, to contend with the cob's excitability, our own nerves and the beasts who seemed not to have been privileged to sniff human flesh ever in their lives before. What with that, the freezing cold and the harum-scarum state of the road, it was timely, nay essential to repair to a hostelry. Before we did so, my companion pointed across to the estuary where the boats had come to take the famine emigrants to America and, momentarily moved by this memory, he said there was a castle not far away, Rahinnane, built by local labour, and that the strength of the mortar was due to the fact that it was mixed in with the blood of the people. Then he made me run a few yards to look at a windmill that was being restored by a group of students and would be a real eye-catcher for tourists because they would be milling flour there next year and the whole world wanted to get back to nature.

Our arrival in the hostelry was somewhat precipitate since they were not ready for early-morning callers even though it was near noon. A pub is one thing at night and another thing altogether in the raw unaerosoled morning. The pyramids of glasses along the counter, a consignment of ashes in the grate and, on the hearth, chairs and stools turned over and the daughter of the house, aged six or seven, playing unmolested on the Moon Patrol video game. The billiard table looked a picture of abandonment and the whole place needed an influx of merry customers. A young boy was engaged in the task of tidying up, but had a desultory approach, his interest being consumed by a video of rock musicians on a television screen which was positioned so high up that it hurt the neck to keep looking at it. The video he had made himself, a *compote* from various programmes, and made more with an eye for frenzy than any notion of continuity. Never mind, my friend of the high-roads was blissfully happy, being now the proud recipient of a pint and a hot toddy, with another on the way and the reins under the leg of the table, and every so often an unholy yell delivered to let the cob know that he hadn't forgotten her and that he was still 'master'.

'You didn't show the white feather,' he kept saying to me, praising my fortitude at coming out at all, my apparent absence of hysteria when the dogs descended on us and my appreciation of the beautiful and ancient countryside. In my heart I was aching to go home, until it suddenly occurred to me that this was home, this country of hills and promontories, this country of stone walls, old oratories, new grottoes, seedy hostelries, lonely schoolhouses, laser discos, automatic milking parlours, tufted islands and people ravenous for company. A shaft of sadness went through me, both at my inability to change things and my refusal to accept them as they are.

'You didn't show the white feather, Edwina,' he kept saying and, now fortified by hot toddies and careless of protocol, he was back to the transports of the previous night, thou'll wife in jail, grabbing one's arse on the mountain and all the heady Dan McGrew bravado.

It would need more than a fleet of mobile libraries to change Ireland. It would need a hundred Sigmund Freuds to unravel the Gordian knots of guilt and anger and darkness and tortuous sex.

The inviolate beauty and the primeval emptiness are all there, in defiance of progress and the march of time. High peninsulas, coves between pillars of jagged rock, slices of sea like jewellery flung in between, teeming clouds over mountains, sometimes in dense mist and occasionally so clear that their peaks are like shelves propping up a sky. In the more arable fields cattle stand in complete immobility, with wisps of straw like streamers of pity and beseech coming out of their mouths. In other fields the grass in tufts, fawn and dun coloured, and forever the crows, the rooks and the magpies swooping and sweeping, giving a semblance of urgency. I asked the driver of the hackney-car why this beauty was so unique, since sea, inlet and mountain are common to so many countries. He thought for a moment and said, 'I could be wrong, I don't have the vocabulary, but I think it's the colouring, it's brown one minute and blue the next and black and purple and indigo. It's liquid, that's what it is, a liquid land.' Or a rainbow, forever forming, forever vanishing. Thackeray said that he couldn't describe it and that big words don't do. Neither do little words. It is an indelibly beautiful country, it is also dolorous, it drastically needs funds, its people need psychological lancing, because in trying to shed the yoke and image of the past they have lost an essential part of themselves – their poetry – not the jibberish that passes for poetry but the true unflinching expression of self. It is as if a great hallucination in the form of mediocrity has spawned itself upon the nation, sapping its vitality, quenching its primordial fire.

VANISHING
IRELAND

25

Ring of Kerry, 1982

Farm scene, Achill Island, 1985

Farmyard hens, 1985

Cottage, Co. Kerry, 1970

Fifteen years later

Connemara couple, 1970

Inside their home

Farmworker's house, Co. Waterford, 1985

Fireside, Co. Waterford, 1985

Traditional fireplace, Co. Kerry, 1985

Brownstown, Co. Waterford, 1985

Peatcutter, Connemara, 1971

Peeling potatoes, Connemara, 1970

Whitewashing, Connemara, 1985

Rainstorm, Connemara, 1970

Peatcutter's bicycle, 1985

Cattle, Co. Mayo, 1976

Milk lorry, Connemara, 1972

Farmstead, Co. Kerry, 1973

Peatcutting, Co. Kerry, 1985

Fishermen with currach, 1985

Achill Island, 1985

Tramore, Co. Waterford, 1985

Irish deckchair, Tramore Beach, Co. Waterford, 1984

52   Celtic crosses, Co. Galway, 1985

Roadside shrine, Co. Waterford, 1984   53

Croagh Patrick, Co. Mayo, 1985

Roadside shrine, Connemara, 1984

The Bargain Stores, Abbeyfeale, 1985

Barber's shop, Sneem, Co. Kerry, 1972   59

60 Co. Galway, 1985

Auction at Listowel Market, Co. Kerry, 1985

Sheep fair, Killarney, Co. Kerry, 1970

Sheep farmers, Kenmare Fair, Co. Kerry, 1969

66   Donkey foal, Killorglin, Co. Kerry, 1971

Horse fair, Killorglin, Co. Kerry, 1971　　67

Puck horse fair, Killorglin, Co. Kerry, 1971

Traditional Puck goat, Killorglin, Co. Kerry, 1971   69

Musician, Co. Galway, 1973

Girl marchers, Listowel, Co. Kerry, 1985

Horse dealers, Killorglin, Co. Kerry, 1971

Farmers, Co. Cork, 1971

Donkey auction, Co. Kerry, 1971

Michael Cliff with fox cub, Co. Kerry, 1985   75

Tinker caravan, Co. Cork, 1982

Tinker family, Co. Waterford, 1973

Father and son, Co. Waterford, 1973   79

Leaving Annestown, Co. Waterford, 1973

Abandoned car, Co. Kerry, 1985

Boy with hurley, 1985

John Joe O'Brien, hurley maker, Co. Tipperary, 1985

John O'Shea, master carpenter, Cahirciveen, Co. Kerry, 1985

Joe Casey, near Sneem, Co. Kerry, 1970

Bodhran maker, Listowel, 1985

Bat Mansfield, blacksmith, Kilmacthomas, Co. Waterford, 1985

Abandoned pony trap, Co. Clare, 1985

Horses and jaunting cart, Inch Beach, Co. Kerry, 1970

Racehorses, Tramore Beach, Co. Waterford, 1985

Co. Kerry, 1972

92   Paddy Quinn in *seanachie* pub, Co. Waterford, 1985

Musicians, Listowel, Co. Kerry, 1985 93

94   Delacey's Bar, Kilmeadan, Co. Waterford, 1972

Musicians, Co. Waterford, 1985

Home entertainment, Co. Kerry, 1985

Tin whistle, Co. Kerry, 1970

Fireside, Co. Galway, 1970

Tom and Kitty Power, Co. Waterford, 1984

Michael Hussey, Co. Kerry, 1970

Fifteen years later

102

Co. Mayo, 1985

Ruin, Co. Kerry, 1985

Farmyard outhouse, Co. Clare, 1982

Empty farmhouse, Co. Clare, 1985

Derelict farmhouse, Brownstown, Co. Waterford, 1985

Abandoned farmhouse, Brownstown, Co. Waterford, 1985

Co. Galway, 1985

Peatcutter's family, Co. Kerry, 1970

Stacked peat, Co. Kerry, 1980

Haymaking, Co. Mayo, 1972

Thatcher, Dunhill, Co. Waterford, 1985

Windowsill, Co. Waterford, 1984 115

Hallway, Tramore, Co. Waterford, 1984

Kitty Power's kitchen, Co. Waterford, 1985

David Gunn and Mary O'Donnell, Co. Kerry, 1985

Bachelor, Co. Kerry, 1970

Peatcutter, Co. Kerry, 1970

Co. Kerry, 1980

James Breen, Co. Kerry, 1985

Dick O'Mahony, saddlemaker, Dungarvan, Co. Waterford, 1985

John O'Shea, Ballinskelligs, Co. Kerry, 1985

General provisions shop, Kenmare, Co. Kerry, 1970

Refugee children, Co. Cork, 1970

128

The O'Shea family, Sneem, Co. Kerry, 1973

Dunhill, Co. Waterford, 1985

Co. Galway, 1973

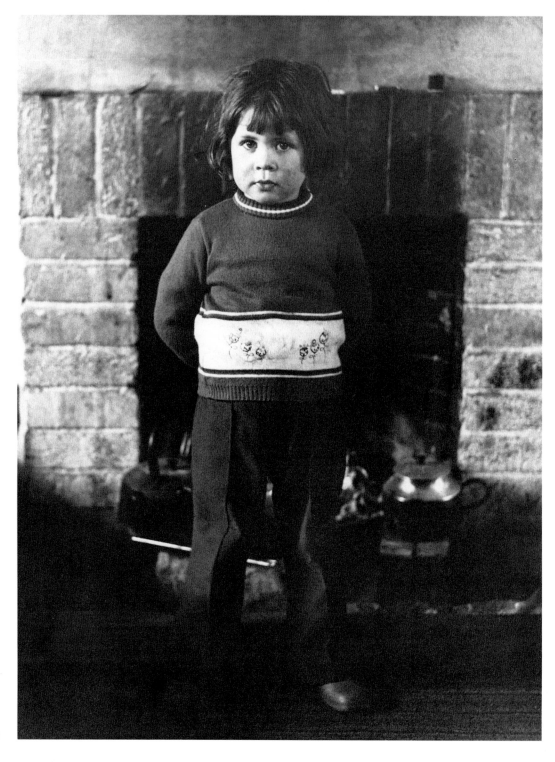

Child, Co. Cork, 1970

Co. Galway, 1985

List of Photographs

Photographing Ireland over the years has become something of a yearly pilgrimage for me, my absence allowing me to see Ireland with the detached eye of a stranger yet knowing it as an insider.

The Ireland I knew as a boy is fast disappearing. When it goes, much of the country's special charm and beauty, so fondly remembered by its emigrants, will be lost for ever. As a photographer I have been drawn to the thatched cottages and the people who hang on to the old ways. They are reminders of my childhood, of the home where I lived with my aunt and uncle after my mother died and my father emigrated. I vividly recall the warmth of the open fireplace and the fun of turning the bellows wheel, the flickering light from the paraffin lamp casting giant shadows around the whitewashed walls. Now these cottages, built of stone and clay in another age, are crumbling beyond repair. The remaining inhabitants, many lonely bachelors, and elderly couples whose sons and daughters have long since emigrated, are slowly dying. Abandoned and decaying homesteads now dot the landscape like ancient monuments to a gentle and kind-hearted people.

The photographs in this book are a tribute to some of them. They are part of a changing world whose unique lifestyle may soon be lost for ever, a vanishing Ireland.

London 1986   Richard Fitzgerald

134

135

Acknowledgments

I would like to express my sincere thanks to the following people who played a major part in the preparation of this book. Firstly the people of rural Ireland for the warmth and kindness shown to me on my many visits; my aunt and uncle, Mai and Tommy Giles, for those early years and the memory of their cottage in Kilmeadan; John and Anne O'Brien, Tramore, for their help and introductions; Julian Heath for his suggestions and general interest in my photography; Ian Craig for design and layout; and finally I am greatly honoured and indebted to Edna O'Brien for her beautiful text.

R.F.

Technical Notes

Photography enthusiasts may wish to know the equipment I used for the photographs in this book. A number of the early photographs were taken on an old Rollie T 2¼ sq. twin lens reflex camera with a 75mm lens. The majority, particularly in recent years, were taken on two Nikon F2 bodies, using mainly 24mm, 85mm and 105mm lenses. I rarely use long tele-photo lenses as I prefer to confront my subjects at close range once permission to take the pictures has been granted. Whenever possible I prefer to work with available light for interior shots since the setting up of elaborate lighting equipment may frighten off many a camera-shy person. As Irish cottages tend to be on the dark side because of their tiny windows, working with available light on a dull day can be a daunting task. For many of my pictures additional light was gained by opening the front and back doors which usually lead off the living area, and uprating the black and white film to 800 ASA. I use Ilford HP5 400 ASA film and process in ID 11 developer. The colour films used were Ektachrome 64 ASA and Fujichrome 100 ASA. I prefer to print all my work myself on Agfa Record Rapid paper.

R.F.

136

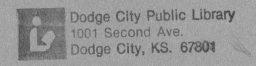